THE RAILROAD SWITCHING TERMINAL AT MAYBROOK, NEW YORK

THE RAILROAD SWITCHING TERMINAL AT MAYBROOK, NEW YORK

GATEWAY TO THE EAST

Marc Newman
with The Maybrook Railroad Historical Society

PURPLE MOUNTAIN PRESS
Fleischmanns, New York

The Railroad Switching Terminal at Maybrook, New York: Gateway to the East

First Edition 2006

Published by
Purple Mountain Press, Ltd.
PO Box 309, Fleischmanns, New York 12430-0309
845-254-4062, 845-254-4476 (fax)
purple@catskill.net
http://www.catskill.net/purple

Copyright © 2006 by Marc Newman and the Maybrook Railroad Historical Society

All rights reserved under International and Pan-American Copyright Conventions.
No part of this book may be reproduced or transmitted by any means
without permission in writing from the publisher.

ISBN 1-930098-69-3

Library of Congress Control Number 2006936057

Manufactured in the United States of America on acid-free paper
5 4 3 2 1

To all the men and women of the Maybrook Switching Terminal,
fifteen hundred employees, who, through hard work and dedication,
maintained the rail service as part of the continental United States.

And to the Maybrook Railroad Historical Society & Museum,
especially Antonio "Tony" Marano, historian and museum president,
and Albert Alexander, humanitarian and philanthropist.
The museum's valuable collection has become an important source
of the history of American railroads.

Special thanks to
Bernie Rudberg for reading the manuscript.

CONTENTS

Introduction
9

1. Railroad Yards
11

2. NYNH&HRR et al.
29

3. Railroad Cars
35

4. Railroad Buildings and Services
43

5. Railroad Employees
51

6. Railroad Machines
65

7. Railroad Tools and Equipment
69

8. In and Around the Rail Yard
83

Introduction

THE CONCEPT of a carriage or wagon on iron rails dates back to the early nineteenth century. Inventors and investors developed different means of energy to pull a wagon on iron rail. Everything from livestock, such as dogs, mules, horses, and oxen, to "wind power" were just a few of the methods used to pull heavy wagons for freight service. Steam-driven railroad service was well established in England in the mid-1820s. While the first steam engine in America traveled from Honesdale to Carbondale in Pennsylvania in 1829 it proved to be too heavy for its wooden tracks and was never used in revenue service. The first railroad service in the United States was by the Baltimore & Ohio Railroad (B&O) between Baltimore and Ellicott Mills, Maryland, in 1830. The decade of the 1830s would see the emergence of rail systems in the eastern United States. Prior to the Civil War, there were hundreds of rail lines, which stretched thousands of miles through the Northeast, Old Northwest, Southeast and part of the South. Erastus Corning of New York created the first railroad system, the New York Central, by the 1850s.

During the Civil War President Abraham Lincoln continued a preliminary plan for a transcontinental railroad. Secretary of War Jefferson Davis (later president of the Confederate States of America) outlined the plan during the Pierce administration, 1853–1857. The Pacific Railroad Act of 1862 led to the creation of the first of several transcontinental railroads. From 1862 to 1869, the Central Pacific Railroad laid track east from Sacramento, California, while the Union Pacific Railroad moved its track lines west from Omaha, Nebraska. On May 10, 1869, both railroad companies met at Promontory, Utah. The "wedding of the rails" united the nation from coast to coast. Other cross-country railroad systems were created in the post-Civil War period. By the end of the nineteenth century, additional transcontinental railroads emerged, including the Great Northern Railroad, the Northern Pacific Railroad, the Santa Fe Railroad, and the Southern Pacific Railroad. Railroad tycoons Edward H. Harriman, Cornelius Vanderbilt, James J. Hill, J. P. Morgan, and others invested millions of dollars in rail expansion. Small railroad companies were either part of the consolidation of these rail conglomerates or were forced to make use of their track lines. During the Civil War, the Union made use of rail lines in the Old Northwest and targeted the destruction of rail centers and major transportation depots that would freight both war supplies and soldiers to the battlefront. The Union army destroyed important rail lines during major battles in places such as Manassas Junction (Bull Run), Vicksburg, Chattanooga, Petersburg, and Atlanta. It was the aftermath of the war that saw the development of additional transcontinental railroads and small rail companies. By the 1870s, Chicago became the largest transportation center of the United States.

A shortage of bridges was one impediment to the growth of rail transportation, especially on the East Coast. The Hudson River divided New England from the rest of the country, and railroad trains had to disconnect their cars and load them on ferries to cross. The extra time and labor made freight transportation costly for businesses and consumers relying on goods by rail in the Northeast. Ferries, such as the one between Newburgh and Dutchess Junction or Fishkill Landing could not operate at all when the Hudson River froze over in winter. This was due to change with the opening of a new railroad bridge at Poughkeepsie in 1888. As the twentieth century dawned, the need for a large switching yard to handle the increased traffic using the bridge became obvious.

A SHORT TIMELINE OF EARLY LOCOMOTIVE DEVELOPMENT

1804
Steam engine used between Penydarren and Abercynon in Welsh coal mines.

1825
Passenger service on the Stockton & Darlington Railway in England.

1829
George Stephenson had nineteen different locomotives built in England by 1829.

1829
The D&H Canal Company ordered a locomotive from England,
but it proved too heavy for their tracks.

1830
The B&O RR began passenger service between Baltimore and Ellicott Mills, Maryland.

1831
The *Best Friend of Charleston* began service in South Carolina.

1831
The Camden & Amboy RR began service in New Jersey.

1831
New York State's first railroad, the Mohawk & Hudson, began service
between Albany and Schenectady.

CHAPTER ONE
Railroad Yards

DURING THE 1850s AND 1860s, suggestions were made to create a bridge across the Hudson River at Poughkeepsie. By 1872, construction began on the Poughkeepsie Railroad Bridge but there were numerous delays. The cornerstone was placed on the west side of the Hudson River in 1873, and the bridge was finally completed in 1888. It was just before New Year's Day 1889 that the very first railroad train crossed the river. A new railroad was also being constructed at this time that connected the western end of the bridge with Orange Junction and Campbell Hall. The operation of floating railroad cars from Newburgh to Fishkill Landing would now be obsolete.

The new railroad bridge measured 6,727 feet in length and stood 212 feet above the Hudson River. The bridge stretched from the western shore at Highland in Ulster County to Poughkeepsie on the eastern shore in Dutchess County. Upon the completion, trains were able to carry freight efficiently from the western states to New England.

In 1889, a single-track line was built from Highland to Orange Junction (later known as Maybrook Junction and then Maybrook). The Philadelphia, Reading & New England Railroad operated the line. Ten years later, the railroad became defunct, and the Central New England took command of the road.

Prior to 1888, four railroads operated from the eastern shore of the Hudson River into Connecticut using ferries to move train cars across the river. When the Poughkeepsie Bridge was completed, the bridge company wanted to buy the Poughkeepsie and Eastern Railroad (P&E) for access to New England,

The Poughkeepsie Railroad Bridge.

The Poughkeepsie Railroad Bridge with train c. 1950s. Courtesy of the Maybrook Railroad Historical Society

but P&E management would not sell. The bridge company then built the Poughkeepsie and Connecticut Railroad in parallel with the P&E and began service into Connecticut. With financial backing from the New Haven Railroad, the Central New England Railway was formed in 1899. The CNE Rwy had purchased the bridge and all of the smaller east-west rail lines, including the ferry, in the early years of the twentieth century. The last train car ferry to Fishkill Landing was in 1904. The Maybrook yard was small in those days, and the railroad terminal fulfilled the needs of both passenger and freight services.

As the Poughkeepsie Railroad Bridge offered access to the East, the new terminal became the gateway for cars loaded with industrial and agricultural goods from the main national terminal at Chicago and coal from Pennsylvania. Cars from Massachusetts and Connecticut going west were either empty or loaded with goods from the factories and farms of New England.

A large two-story building was constructed at the end of Main Street in Maybrook for the administrative office of the Central New England Railway. The terminal consisted of a few liner tracks for receiving trains from western railroads and a few liner tracks for receiving New England trains delivered to western lines. During the period from 1889 to 1903, the Central New England Railroad maintained the terminal with six tracks, an enginehouse, and a turntable at the Old Row area of company housing.

The Central New England built the houses

The high trestle of the Poughkeepsie Bridge.
Courtesy of the Maybrook Railroad Historical Society

that made up the Old Row to accommodate its permanent employees. The Orange County Railroad also maintained a few tracks for receiving and delivering trains to the Central New England Railway. The Orange County Railroad, later to be known as the Lehigh and Hudson Railroad, maintained a small roundhouse and turntable. This railroad built residential homes for its employees in the area later to be known as "The Lehigh Hill." A large administration building was erected at the site of the old Hallock Lumber Company. This building was centrally located between western railroads and the Lehigh and Hudson yard.

In 1906, the New York, New Haven and Hartford acquired half the interest in the Central New England operation at Orange Junctionand and in less than ten years, assumed full control of the terminal's operations. (The life-span of the Central New England Railroad extended from 1899 to 1927, at which time the New York, New Haven & Hartford Railroad absorbed it). By 1908, plans were underway to construct a huge switching terminal, which would be the largest of its kind east of the Mississippi River. The terminal would enjoy the convenience of repair shops of all kinds, including machine shops, carpenter shops, boxcar repair and rebuilding shops, enginehouse and steam engine rebuilding, a twenty-seven-stall roundhouse, with a ninety-five-foot turntable, a new general office building, a freight transfer platform, a YMCA, and an administration building. An ice manufacturing plant serviced refrigerator cars, and two reservoirs supplied the water needed for it. The icehouse provided both ice blocks and crushed ice for the trains and their cargo. The car repair building was one of the largest shops on the grounds. The terminal took up an area over three miles in length and one mile in width and could handle thousands of cars at the same time. The switching facility was put into operation in 1912.

The new terminal was designed to handle eastbound trains and westbound trains separately. Thus, all the switching and assembling of trains heading east was completely independent from that of trains heading west. Parallel to the rail terminal was Goodwill Road, later called Homestead Avenue and Route 208. The design of the terminal provided a direct and single independent main line used solely for passenger train operations. A passenger station was located at the end of Main Street.

The new freight center was self-sustaining. It had facilities for building boxcars and steam engines, as well as carpenter shops, machine

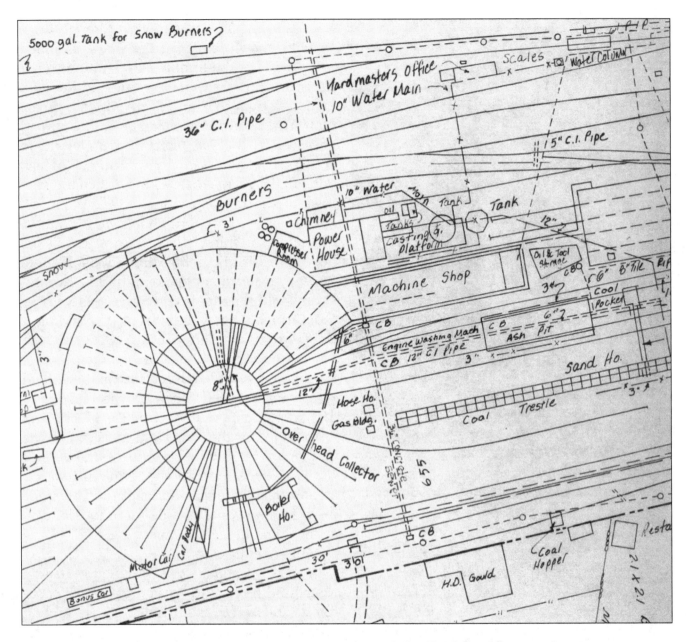

Above: CNERR blueprint with roundhouse turntable.
Courtesy of the Maybrook Railroad Historical Society and Doug Barbiero

Facing page

Top left: CNERR Blueprint of the office and tracks.
Courtesy of the Maybrook Railroad Historical Society and Doug Barbiero

Top right: CNERR blueprint of icehouse and shops.
Courtesy of the Maybrook Railroad Historical Society and Doug Barbiero

Below: The reservoir that supplied water to the enginehouse and powerhouse.
Courtesy of the Maybrook Railroad Historical Society

Railroad Yards

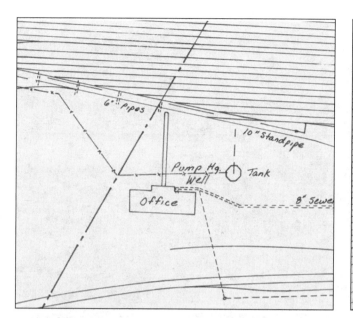

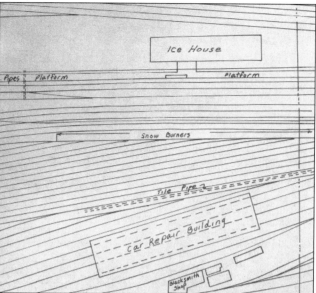

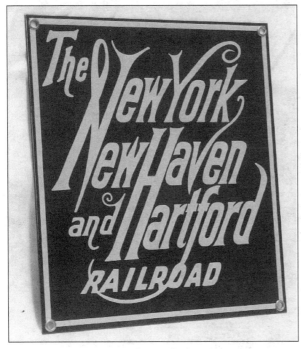

Top: The Maybrook rail yards and roundhouse.
Courtesy of the Maybrook Railroad Historical Society, Ralph Aiello, and Albert Alexander

Above left: A New York, New Haven & Hartford Railroad sign.

Above right: The Maybrook rail yards, including the car shop, rip track, and icing facilities.
Both courtesy of the Maybrook Railroad Historical Society

**Above: Boxcars on track. Below: A view from the water tower.
Both courtesy of the Maybrook Railroad Historical Society**

Above: En route to the eastbound departure yard. Courtesy of Peter C. McLachlan, photographer

Facing page, top: Cabooses and boxcars on the track. Middle: An engine with boxcars and flatcars. Bottom: The eastbound hump with boxcars. All courtesy of the Maybrook Railroad Historical Society

shops, a blacksmith shop, and an ice plant. Today, the southern border would be Route 208 and the northern border Route 17K. All the tracks, if put end to end, would stretch seventy-two miles and would have a capacity of five thousand cars. During World War II, the terminal employed fifteen hundred workers with a weekly payroll of $150,000. In May 1943, a switching record was established. During one twenty-four hour period, 25 eastbound trains (1,665 cars) and 29 westbound trains (1,826 cars), for a total of 3,491 cars, were switched and assembled into trains.

The switching yards were designed in such a way to keep the cars moving constantly in the same direction until their arrival at the opposite end, where they would await movement to the final destination. The administrative office, keeping records of car movement, was situated in the center of the terminal.

Trains arriving from the west were sent to the eastbound receiving yard, pushed over a gravity hump into a classification yard, gathered together with other cars destined for New England and placed in a train in the eastbound departure yard. Westbound trains followed a similar network of receiving and departure yards.

The hump was a rise that used gravity to move the cars into the classification yard. An engine pushed cars to the hump and then, after the pin was pulled to separate them, let gravity take them down into the classification yard and to a designated track. The westbound hump would sometimes switch trains of 150 cars. A brakeman rode each car into the yard and used the brake to slow it as it reached its destination. Two "rip" (repair in place) tracks were used for minor repairs on the cars. Workers waited in the shanties near the humps for the next train to arrive. The eastbound hump was higher than the westbound hump.

Both eastbound and westbound yards were composed of three smaller yards. The receiving yard cataloged the arrival of all

trains. It contained a total of eight receiving tracks. Upon their arrival at Maybrook, car inspectors checked the trains for any defects or missing parts. Cars found to have problems were tagged with a card marked "bad order" and were switched out for the car repair shop. In the meantime, the incoming train conductor dropped off a bundle of car waybills at the small yard office.

Many of the trains carried farm goods and beef from the Midwest. Others carried coal, the main supply of home and factory heating, especially in New England and New York. Many of the boxcars and flatcars that arrived in the eastbound receiving yard had journeyed across the United States. Some had traveled along the Great Northern Railroad and its rival line, the Northern Pacific. After traveling to the Midwest, the cars were detached and then coupled to engines that carried them east.

The eastbound hump was the end of a "funnel" of seven tracks from the eastbound receiving yard. There, workmen unhitched each car and "rode" it onto elevated hump. Sometimes these cars, with a brakeman on the roof, would reach speeds of thirty miles per hour, moving from the elevated area to a specific track in the classification yard. The cars, with the exception of the engines and cabooses, were then switched into one of the twenty classification tracks to be processed for movement or repair.

The classification yardmaster ordered a switch engine and crew to assemble certain trains for the New England area from various tracks in the yard. The train was then pulled into the eastbound departure yard, which had seven tracks. In the departure yard, the car inspector crew connected air hoses from car to car, pumped in air up to a certain pressure, and then inspected the train for air leaks.

Having been fueled, the engine was taken from either the enginehouse yard or the roundhouse and attached with a caboose. The caboose track was in front of the main office. When there were three to five cabooses near the administration building, they were turned around and used for scheduled trains or extra trains.

The yard switcher then connected the caboose to the rear of the train. After the conductor received his train list and waybills from the main office, a road engine was coupled to the head end and a pusher crew was called in to help the train depart.

A large water reservoir stood adjacent to the eastbound departure yard. The reservoir was built to supply water for steam engines and the powerhouse and to clean ashes from steam engines. After 1924, when the icehouse was built, the reservoir water was also used to make ice for refrigerator cars from the west that carried vegetables and other types of produce.

The westbound railroad yard had three yards identical to those of the eastbound yard and seven receiving tracks. Trains leaving the westbound departure yard headed toward terminals in Pennsylvania and Illinois.

The length of trains increased from ten cars originally to fifty cars and, later, to one hundred cars as the engines increased in power. The total tonnage also increased from seven hundred tons to over seven thousand tons. Many trains were routed from Maybrook to Newtown, Connecticut, and then to Cedar Hill, Connecticut, for points farther east. Cedar Hill had the largest freight yard in Connecticut. Trains passed through Danbury to

Facing page: The eastbound departure yard. Top: With cars. Middle: With steel girders perhaps destined for building Interstate 91 or 95. Bottom: Note the reservoir. Courtesy of the Maybrook Railroad Historical Society

22   *The Railroad Switching Terminal*

other cities along the eastern route, including Bridgeport and New Haven, Connecticut, and Worcester and Boston, Massachusetts.

The Maybrook yards had some 119 switches, and the whole terminal had approximately seventy-eight to eighty miles of track. Cars that were in need of repair at the car shop were placed on one of two rip tracks. Once the cargo of each car was examined, cargo content was unloaded and platform workers used a hand truck to load it onto designated cars. Certain cargoes, such as onions, potatoes, and some machinery, were weighed by scale. The cargo was taken off the car and placed on the scale shed. A scale-test car was used periodically to ensure that the scale was in proper working order. After the cars were stocked or restocked, they were sealed and sent to the crossover track where the car would be coupled to a train leaving the westbound or eastbound departure yards.

From 1890 to the 1920s, passenger trains traveled along the perimeter of the terminal, out of view from any freight switching operations. Daily passenger trains operated from Hartford, Connecticut, to Campbell Hall, New York, making connections with the Ontario & Western Railway (O&W) and other western lines. Several different railroad companies made use of the Maybrook Switching Terminal. Boston to Washington, DC, passenger trains ran through Maybrook before World War I.

Facing page, top: Leaving Maybrook for Hartford. Middle: The 0414 diesel train leaving Cedar Hill for Maybrook. Bottom: The 1222 leaving Maybrook for Newtown. All courtesy of Peter C. McLachlan, photographer

Above: Locomotives in the westbound arrival yard.
Courtesy of the Maybrook Railroad Historical Society and Sam Christiano

Below, left: A detached engine. Courtesy of the Maybrook Railroad Historical Society

Below, right: The Extra 0409 westbound from Connecticut. Courtesy of Peter C. McLachlan, photographer

Above: The westbound hump with shed, and torch light. Courtesy of the Maybrook Railroad Historical Society

Right: The 0410 westbound to Maybrook from Connecticut. Courtesy of Peter C. McLachlan, photographer

Below: An engine & coal tender pushing boxcars on the hump. Courtesy of the Maybrook Railroad Historical Society and Sam Christiano

A New York, New Haven & Hartford train. Courtesy of Peter C. McLachlan, photographer

Top: The westbound departure yard. Courtesy of the Maybrook Railroad Historical Society

Right: A train at the trestle bridge.

Below: A New York, New Haven & Hartford train.

Courtesy of Peter C. McLachlan, photographer

A departing Lehigh & New England train. Courtesy of the Maybrook Railroad Historical Society

CHAPTER TWO
NYNH&HRR et al.

THE CENTRAL NEW ENGLAND RAILway Company took control of the rail line that was controlled by the Philadelphia, Readubg & New England Railroad and established a small terminal at Orange Junction (Maybrook). The terminal consisted of a few tracks for the westbound trains and a few tracks for the eastbound trains with a small roundhouse to service and repair train engines. Central New England constructed a two-story administration building and made living quarters available for its permanent workers.

Many railroads made use of the Maybrook Switching Terminal, including the New York, New Haven & Hartford, the Ontario & Western, the New York Central, the Erie (Erie Lackawanna), the Lehigh & New England, and the Lehigh & Hudson. The Lehigh & Hudson

Central New England's # 33. Courtesy of the Maybrook Railroad Historical Society

Railroad was an important freight service for traffic to and from New England. By 1882, the Lehigh & Hudson River Railway Company and the Warwick Valley Railroad Company had merged to form the Lehigh & Hudson Railway Company. The Lehigh & New England Railroad organized the Orange County Railroad Company in the late 1880s. That company shipped services and goods such as anthracite and bituminous coal, farm perishables, iron, steel, and petroleum, especially from Easton, Pennsylvania, to Maybrook. Before the mid-1890s, the Lehigh & New England Railroad was the Pennsylvania, Poughkeepsie & Boston Railroad. By the late 1890s, the newly created Lehigh & New England laid track from New Jersey to Campbell Hall, which connected to the Erie Railroad tracks. After the completion of the Poughkeepsie Bridge, the Lehigh & New England delivered coal and steel from Allentown and Bethlehem, Pennsylvania, through the Maybrook yard. Before the 1950s, the Lehigh & New England Railroad had converted its engines from coal to diesel. During the height of its operation, the company freighted services through portions of northern New Jersey, crossing the Delaware River at the bridge between Portland, Pennsylvania, and Columbia, New Jersey.

Through a series of interchanges with the Lackawanna and the New York, Susquehanna & Western, the Lehigh & New England was able to make use of the Maybrook yard. Unlike many other railroads, the Lehigh & New England used the Maybrook terminal exclusively for freight service and had no passenger service. In the late 1950s, the Lehigh & New England Railroad Company downsized its operations. By 1961, the company had closed. Parts of the line were sold to other railroads, and the New Jersey Central Company and Conrail used other portions of it.

Many of the Erie Railroad trains shipped coal cars from the mines of Scranton and Wilkes-Barre, Pennsylvania. Shipped east, the coal cars were returned empty to their original destination to receive anthracite or bituminous coal. The trains were given special priority during World War II, as there was substantial need for coal as a source of energy and heat on the home front. In the mid-1950s, the Erie Railroad, the Delaware, Hudson Railroad, and the Lackawanna Railroad began discussing the possibility of a merger that would eliminate the competition between the railroad companies. In 1959, the Erie and the Lackawanna Railroad decided to merge their rail lines, and the Erie moved its operation center from Jersey City to Hoboken, New Jersey. The merger, however, did not sustain the success of the Erie Lackawanna, which made use of the Maybrook terminal for some ten years. The railroad, like many in the region, decreased or abandoned its passenger service and relied heavily on freight. Gradually, fuel use in railroad engines and in heating shifted away from coal, decreasing the demand. In the mid-1970s, the Erie Lackawanna Railroad became part of the Conrail system.

Other railroad companies had made use of the facilities of the Maybrook terminal. One important building that employed the largest number of employees was the car repair shop.

Facing page, clockwise from top left: 1.) A New York, New Haven & Hartford train, c. 1940s. Courtesy of the Maybrook Railroad Historical Society 2.) A Lehigh & New England engine. Courtesy of the Maybrook Railroad Historical Society and Charles Davis Sr., photographer 3.) Erie diesel engine F. Courtesy of the Maybrook Railroad Historical Society O&W engines. Courtesy of Peter C. McLachlan. photographer 4.) A Lehigh & New England diesel train. Courtesy of the Maybrook Railroad Historical Society 5.) An Erie engine #712. Courtesy of the Maybrook Railroad Historical Society 6.) Steam engine 1407, class 4-6-4. Courtesy of the Maybrook Railroad Historical Society and Frank Amodio

The Railroad Switching Terminal

Railroad companies such as the New York Central Railroad and the Ontario & Western Railroad (O&W) had their boxcars repaired in the Maybrook yard. The New York & Oswego Midland Railroad served portions of central New York State. The company was purchased and renamed the New York, Ontario & Western Railway in the late 1870s. It was incorporated in 1882 and took over the New York & Oswego Midland Railroad, which was bankrupt. The northern terminal of the New York, Ontario & Western was at Lake Ontario at Oswego, the end of the line. The southern terminal was at Weehawken, New Jersey, with the main freight line from Scranton, Pennsylvania, to Cadosia. The O&W had branches of their lines in Kingston, New York, Monticello, New York, and Port Jervis, New York, to name a few. Through the use of tracks in the Lackawanna Valley, the Ontario & Western shipped large amounts of coal and milk to New York. By 1957, the Ontario & Western had gone out of business.

Industrialist Cornelius Vanderbilt bought the New York & Harlem Railroad, the Hudson River Railroad and the Central Railroad Company in the post Civil War years. The three railroads became the New York Central Railroad, commonly called the grand central railroad, with its main terminal in New York City. The New York Central ran on the east side of the Hudson River from New York City to Albany and west to Chicago. On the west side of the Hudson River, trains ran from Weehawken, New Jersey, to Selkirk and west. The train went to Kingston and Campbell Hall, New York, for the interchange with the New Haven Railroad line, the Erie, and the O&W. Engines and cars of the New York Central in need of repair were brought into the Maybrook terminal from nearby Campbell Hall. After 1973, Penn Central Railroad owned and controlled the New York Central.

The New York, New Haven & Hartford Railroad controlled and maintained the Maybrook Switching Terminal. The New Haven Railroad established its routes as early as the 1820s, the decade of birth for rail development in the United States. In the years prior to the Civil War, many small railroad companies had freight and passenger service in southern New England. The two largest commercial centers in the region were New York City and Boston. In 1872, the New York New Haven Railroad and the Hartford New Haven Railroad merged to create a service to and from Boston and New York. The New York, New Haven & Hartford Railroad controlled more than two thousand miles of track through portions of Rhode Island, Massachusetts, Connecticut, and New York. The J. P. Morgan Trust & Loan Company, along with other investors, gained control of the railroad in 1903. Decades later, at the end of the 1960s, the New York, New Haven & Hartford (New Haven Railroad) became part of the Penn Central Railroad. Several years later, Conrail took over the freight service portions of the New Haven Railroad and the Penn Central, and Amtrak, along with several other companies, took over the passenger service.

It was a holiday in Maybrook when the Ringling Brothers, Barnum & Bailey Circus arrived at the terminal. School was closed by order of the principal and the Maybrook Board of Education. Through the streets of

Facing page, top left: The circus train being inspected. Right: Train 0706, c. 1950s
Middle right: The elephant boxcar. Left: A New York, New Haven & Hartford engine, c. 1960s.
Bottom: Elephants unloaded from boxcar.
All courtesy of the Maybrook Railroad Historical Society

Maybrook, along Tower Avenue and Homestead Avenue, and a host of other small streets, circus employees, including the famous clown Emmett Kelley, entertained the children. For many young residents, the day the circus came to town was one of the greatest moments of growing up in Maybrook. Children went to the railroad yard to see the elephants, giraffes, horses, and other livestock being taken out of the boxcars. They were even allowed to feed and water some of the animals. Other residents walked along the main street and talked to the circus performers like the Tall Man and the Fat Lady. Stores were well stocked with products before the circus arrived. The layover was a financial windfall for local business, as circus employees replenished their supplies and enjoyed the hospitality of the community. In the early and late evening, when the bars and restaurants were crowded with circus employees, residents young and old peeked through the windows to get a glimpse of the men and women who were part of the Greatest Show on Earth.

On Route 208 northbound, a New York State historic marker indicates that in the early part of the twentieth century, Maybrook was the "Largest Railroad Terminal." A sign in the village announces that this was the "Gateway to the East," meaning New England. The Maybrook terminal not only employed most of the residents of the community but also provided valuable services to eastbound and westbound trains.

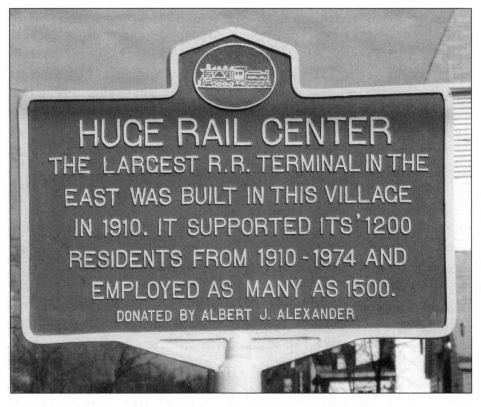

The historic marker.
Courtesy of the Maybrook Railroad Historical Society and Albert J. Alexander

CHAPTER THREE
Railroad Cars

THE HARTFORD & CONNECTICUT western train was the first passenger train to cross the Poughkeepsie Bridge and create rail service over the Hudson River. Early trains had few cars in the 1830s, but by the 1960s, the trains had some well in excess of one hundred cars with locomotives that were diesel electric. The steam engine was commonly called the "iron horse." In the beginning, railroads focused on passenger service, and the number of cars in a passenger train were far fewer than the number in the freight trains of a century later. During the Jacksonian era, the Baltimore & Ohio became the first to build a railroad for passengers, and that railroad became the model on which later ones were based.

Water is poured into the coal tender in preparation for the engine to leave the enginehouse and be coupled to the cars waiting to be taken out of the Maybrook departure yard. In a period of more than one hundred years, some forty thousand steam engines were built for American rail companies. By the late 1940s and into the 1950s, the diesel engine locomotive had replaced many of these steam engines. The diesel locomotive had a specific body design, referred to as the E-Class body shell that was standard in the 1950s and 1960s.

Although the diesel had been developed in the late 1930s, production to replace steam locomotives did not begin until the late 1940s. Diesel engines used both diesel fuel and electric generators. The Baldwin Company designed its engine to look like a shark, and those engines were called Sharknoses. The diesel engine was considered a major improvement over the steam locomotive. It started up very quickly compared to the steam locomotive, which needed time for the boilers to get up a head of steam to create the pressure to move the drive pistons that activated the drive rods that turned the wheels. The diesel engine also required less maintenance and fewer repairs, which led to a reduction in the number of employees in the enginehouse. The three types of diesel locomotives were switch locomotives used in the freight yard, passenger locomotives, with approximately three thousand horsepower, and freight locomotives, with approximately four thousand horsepower. Some of the diesel-electric engines built after the 1970s provide more than six thousand horsepower. These low-maintenance engines can pull a large number of cars and maintain very high speed. The diesel-electric engine makes use of diesel fuel

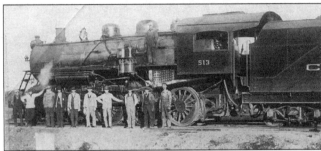

Clockwise from the top:

The first passenger train to cross the Poughkeepsie Bridge, c. 1889.

A Central New England steam engine.

A model train, diesel-electric locomotive. Dan Green, photographer

Central New England's 513 locomotive and tender.

A switch locomotive.

An Erie diesel locomotive.

All courtesy of the Maybrook Railroad Historical Society

with electric generators to develop the power to move hundreds of tons of cars and their contents over great distances. Today, diesel engines power more than ninety percent of U.S. industrial transportation, including rail, boat, truck, bus, and tractor.

The switch locomotive was the smallest of the engines and had approximately two thousand horsepower. The switch engine was used for short-distance hauling and for pulling a small number of cars. In the Maybrook terminal, this engine was used predominantly in the freight yards. Its main purpose was to disassemble trains that entered the arrival yards. An important engine in the switching terminal, it was also used to assemble trains moving from the classification yards to the departure yards.

The coal tender was essential for the steam engine. Located behind the locomotive, the tender had several compartments for storing coal and water. The tender's water tank was filled before the trip and then refilled along the way. Originally, the tender stockpiled cords of wood, which the fireman fed into the furnace of the engine. Wood was used until coal furnaces were developed for the engine.

Trains that entered the Maybrook terminal contained many types of cars. The most dominant type were boxcars. Some trains had as many as one hundred boxcars, all of which had to be classified and sent to New England destinations. The boxcars were then taken to the departure yard, coupled with an engine and a caboose, and sent on to their next destination. Although the structure and dimensions of all boxcars were very similar, some were designated to carry particular contents. The boxcars the New York, New Haven & Hartford Railroad owned were about forty feet long (a few were fifty feet) and had a capacity of sixty-two tons, which was the load limit. The railroad had some three thousand

Model train cars, from the top: boxcar, flatcar, tank car, potatoe boxcar, refrigerator car.

Courtesy of the Maybrook Railroad Historical Society and Dan Green, photographer

Above: A New Haven freight engine 3341. Courtesy of the Maybook Railroad Historical Society

Right: An automobile flatcar. Courtesy of the Maybrook Railroad Historical Society

boxcars, which were used to ship products across the country. The boxcars were loaded with all types of products including small machinery, paper goods, candy, hardware, Stanley tools, Remington guns, sewing machines, and all sorts of clothing, merchandise and canned goods.

Flatcars were modified to accommodate the type of product they were to carry. The deep-well flatcar was used to haul such products as boxed light machinery and transformers. The piggyback flatcar had a tractor trailer box on top and carried machinery, steel girders, pipes, heavy reels of copper wire, and other products. The New York, New Haven & Hartford Railroad had tankers to transport liquids such as diesel oil, lubrication oil, and liquid calcium chloride. Large tank cars were used to transport bunker oil from barges and boats, and some of these cars supplied oil for the powerhouses in Maybrook. Among the other liquids that were shipped were fish oils, animal oils, chlorine, alcohol, propane, and fertilizer.

Insulated boxcars were used especially for the shipment of products from New England, such as Maine potatoes, apples, or grapes. To prevent spoilage of these products while they were being shipped across the country, the cars had to be insulated. Before the use of mechanical refrigerator cars, crushed ice and salt kept meat cars cool, and produce cars were cooled with block ice and ventilators. In later years, refrigerator cars were mechanically cooled to temperatures as low as zero degrees Fahrenheit and below. During the winter, charcoal burners heated the refrigerator cars.

Along with boxcars and flatcars, there were many other types of cars in a train. Coal

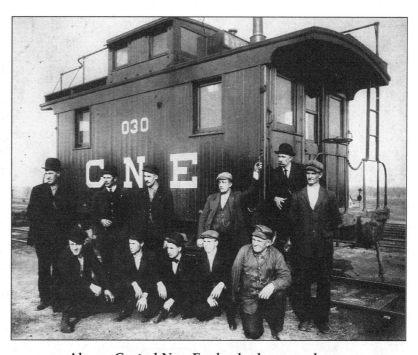

**Above: Central New England caboose and crew.
Below: A caboose bench bed.
Both courtesy of the Maybrook Railroad Historical Society**

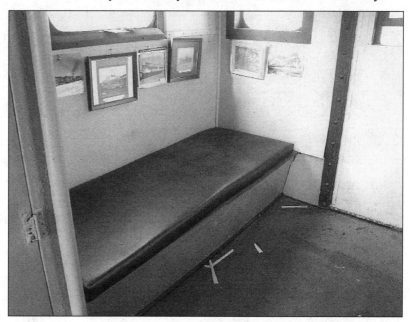

Above: A model train caboose.
Dan Green, photographer.
Left: A caboose stove, table, and storage compartment.
Below. A caboose bunk bed.
Courtesy of the Maybrook Railroad Historical Society

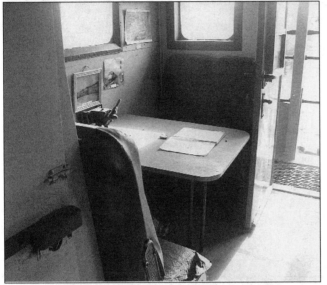

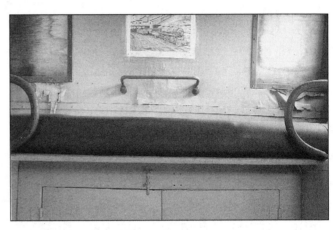

hoppers carried anthracite and bituminous coal and cement hoppers transported material used for making cement for construction work. Open gondolas held large bulk items, and covered gondolas protected large machinery from the elements. Covered hoppers carried grain and automobile flatcars transported motor vehicles. Trains that had all of the same type of car were called solid trains, for example tank car trains, coal hopper trains, or boxcar trains.

Generally located at the rear of a freight train, the caboose carried the crews. On local trains, the caboose was sometimes located behind the diesel engine, with cars behind it, but on long freight trains, it was at the end. A caboose was used on work trains and tool trains. When a train entered the rail yard, the engine and the caboose were detached from the cars, which were then sent to the classification yards.

Four members of the train crew used the facilities of the caboose, including the rear brakeman, rear conductor, engineer, and flagman. Two benches served as beds for two of the men. One door was in the front, and the other door was in the back between the two bench beds. A stove was located at the front of the caboose opposite the table and benches near the door. It burned chunks of coal and provided more than enough heat, even during the coldest winter months. On top of the stove was a flat plate on which the men heated food and beverages during the trip. Next to the stove was an ash pit and a coal bucket and shovel to remove the ashes. The caboose table served many purposes. Important train documents were checked and signed on it. Meals and beverages were served on it. Games of cards were played on it. Each door led to a platform with steps.

Opposite the stove were the bench seats, which had a capacity for four. A third or more of the interior of the caboose consisted of storage lockers with shelving and a closet on one side and toilet facilities on the other side. The cabinets on both sides had numerous shelves for clothing, tools, food, beverages, and other personal possessions of the crew. A bunk bed was on top of each mid-caboose storage. Used by the crew, the two beds were located opposite one another and crew members had to climb onto the shelf and over the bed rail to access the bed. Pillows and blankets were stored in compartments or under the beds.

Located not far from the stove, the bunk beds were a warm place to sleep. Crew members slept after the train reached its destination and was put on the caboose track. While moving, they sat in the cupola to observe the train as it went around bends and to watch for sparks, smoke, and fire. They also looked to the rear for indications of dragging equipment or a wheel off. This would show on ties or in the snow in winter. If a train stopped, a flagman would be dispatched a safe distance to protect the rear from oncoming trains.

The caboose was generally placed at the rear of the train and would display a red flag or light indicating it was the last car.

CHAPTER FOUR
Railroad Buildings and Services

THE CENTRAL NEW ENGLAND roundhouse originally had five stalls, a small turntable, and a track leading from part of the yard to this building. Under the New York, New Haven & Hartford Railroad, the Maybrook roundhouse was enlarged from nine stalls to twenty-seven stalls with a turntable that was almost one hundred feet in length. By the 1920s, the economic boom of the decade encouraged both passenger and freight service. Middle class citizens were traveling to various parts of the country, as many businesses had employees working eight to ten hours a day, five days a week. The mass production of radios, cars, iceboxes, washing machines, and so on encouraged the transportation of these products by rail. The roundhouse was used for servicing and repairing railroad engines. The engine was disconnected from the train in the receiving yard or the arrival yard and sent via designated tracks directly to the roundhouse, where it was rotated on the turntable and left in a vacant stall. Steam locomotives were repaired and a special crew serviced their boilers.

Many steam engine service jobs were gradually eliminated as steam locomotives were phased out. However, the roundhouse was still heavily used for servicing and maintaining diesel engines. The decade of the 1950s was a very active one for Maybrook employees as the United States began to recover from recession in the aftermath of World War II. Young men returning from Europe or the Pacific theater were able to get jobs in the shop buildings, the roundhouse, and the enginehouse.

The roundhouse and turntable were part of the enginehouse complex, a series of buildings in which highly skilled craftsmen, including boilermakers, welders, and blacksmiths repaired engines and engine parts. The enginehouse also included a blacksmith shop and a wheel shop in which engine wheels were replaced or repaired and ball bearings were changed or adjusted. Fire cleaners maintained the steam engines by shaking out the old ashes and clinkers (coal rocks with a large amount of iron, which made the ashes stick together) into the ash pit. The clinkers, which hardened as they cooled, sometimes had to be broken up and dropped through the firebox

Facing page top: The roundhouse interior. Bottom: Steam locomotive 3206.
Both courtesy of the Maybrook Railroad Historical Society

Top: The roundhouse. Above: The ashpit. Both courtesy of the Maybrook Railroad Historical Society

and into the ash pit. Located near the roundhouse, the ash pit was about one hundred feet long and twenty-five feet wide. The "clam digger" dug out the ashes and used the cinders for ballast and fill under the tracks.

The Maybrook roundhouse had tracks that went around and tracks that went into the roundhouse. In the early days, when the facility was small, the turntable was cranked by hand to move the locomotive around and onto a specific track leading to a vacant stall. Years later, under the management and control of the New York, New Haven & Hartford Railroad, the turntable was mechanized and more stalls were added to accommodate the growing number of trains using the Maybrook terminal. Sometimes, children of the employees, such as little Cindy Yanello, sat with a parent in the cab of a locomotive on the turntable while it spun several times. For those lucky youngsters, it was like being on a carousel at the park or fairground.

Similar to a car jack, the Whiting Hoist with the crane was used in the enginehouse to lift up steam engines to work on repairs underneath the locomotive or to remove and replace the wheels. In order to inspect its firebox, the engine had to be lifted into the air. Among the workers whose jobs involved the Whiting Hoist were steamfitters, electricians, steelworkers, and welders. The hoist was capable of lifting a 125- to 150-ton engine. Once the engine was up in the air, workers changed some of the rods and the pistons.

The car repair shop was the largest and one of the most important buildings in the terminal. This shop was for the repair of boxcars, flatbed cars, and refrigerator cars. When trains arrived in the rail yard, the inspectors deadheaded the cars that were in need of repair.

A steam locomotive and a coal tender on the turntable. Courtesy of the Maybrook Railroad Historical Society

The cars were separated from the train and sent on designated tracks directly to the car shop. The car shop employed a crew of several dozen specialized employees. The car shop had four tracks leading into the building, which accommodated as many as forty or fifty cars. It had a paint shop with pipe maintenance men and stencil painters who painted the cars and lettered them with the railroad name or logo. Carpenters repaired the flooring and replaced the doors of the boxcars. Workmen inspected and repaired the air brakes.

The truck shop was a separate department within the car shop. The truck consisted of the two axles at either end of the boxcar. Truck repairmen fixed any defect or impairment on the axle or the wheels. Many of the men who worked in the car shop were general repairmen who moved from one project to another within the various departments. Others were highly specialized and worked only on specific jobs. The machine shop was another department that

The engine house with diesel engines. Courtesy of the Maybrook Railroad Historical Society and Robbie Brown Sr.

specialized in making metal parts and replacement parts for engines, boxcars, and cabooses.

From the early 1900s to the 1950s, the Maybrook terminal serviced steam locomotive trains. The engines of these large trains required three ingredients, including coal, water, and sand. Coal was burned in the furnace to heat the water in the boiler. The boiling water created steam pressure, which was the force that moved the pistons and rods that turned the wheels of the train. Sand was placed at the top of the engine, where the heat dried it out, enabling it to flow through pipes underneath the wheels and create traction. The coal trestle was attached to the buildings on an incline, which was filled with coal. The trestle reached coal tenders on three tracks. Some compartments in the tenders were filled with coal and other compartments were filled with water. The big engines had stokers who air-sprayed coal around the firebox. The smaller engines had firemen who shoveled coal into the firebox. Although most steam engines burned coal, some burned oil. Along with tons

The Whiting hoist. Courtesy of Peter C. McLachlan, photographer

The car repair shop. Courtesy of the Maybrook Railroad Historical Society

The car repair shop with boxcars. Courtesy of the Maybrook Railroad Historical Society

The back storage lot. Courtesy of the Maybrook Railroad Historical Society and C. Davis Sr., photographer

of coal, steam engines consumed large amounts of water. Water from the terminal's storage tank was filtered through an underground pipe and pumped into the standpipe. Using the spout of the standpipe, the fireman filled the water compartments on the tenders. During the trip, the fireman monitored the engine's water gauge. When the needle dropped below a certain point or temperature, he used the water valve to transfer water from the tender to the engine boiler.

The administration building was the control center for all incoming trains. During the day shift, as many as thirty employees worked here, including the trainmaster, general yardmaster, railroad agent, chief clerks, clerks, secretaries, and others. After reviewing the waybills and manifests, the staff decided where each train should go. These decisions were passed along to the yardmaster, who gave the orders to the train crew.

Another area in the rail yard was a manmade reservoir that provided ice for the refrigerator boxcars. The ice was loaded in blocks and crushed to use for preserving perishable items such as meat and fish. The icehouse was closed after trains started using

The Central New England machine shop.

The coal trestle and the sand pile.

At the coal trestle.

All courtesy of the Maybrook Railroad Historical Society

new refrigerator cars with built-in cooling units. The loading platforms were another area of construction. Cargo was unloaded from the boxcars onto platforms or docks. There, it was inspected and reassigned to other cars or loaded onto trucks to be delivered within the region. The platform crew consisted of three men, including a checker, a loader, and a trucker. Separate from the crew were the stevedores who loaded some of the freight on the cars.

There were three dozen small buildings or shacks, sometimes called shanties, located throughout the the Maybrook terminal. There were three buildings in each of the receiving and departure yards and several by each of the humps. In between jobs, the switch tenders, maintenance-of-way men, car inspectors, and other workers used the potbelly stove-heated shacks, especially in the winter.

In the early days of the Maybrook terminal, workers who needed sleeping accommodations stayed in local boardinghouses. Later, the Central New England Railroad made several bungalows available. After the New York, New Haven & Hartford took over the terminal, the increase in the number of employees needing

Coming through the coal trestle.

The coal and sand service area.

A railroad platform used by the icehouse gang to service refridgerator cars.

All courtesy of the Maybrook Railroad Historical Society

Railroad Buildings and Services

The administration building.
Transfer platform.
The fire shack.
All courtesy of the Maybrook Railroad Historical Society

overnight housing led to the construction of a YMCA. By the 1940s, the YMCA had enlarged its services to include food service and a gymnasium. Although some of the railroad workers had little time to go to the gymnasium, Maybrook teenagers used the facilities for sports and team competitions, and young and old held dances and other social activities there.

50   The Railroad Switching Terminal

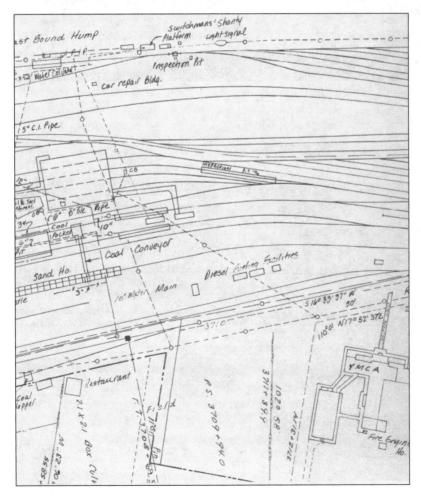

Top: The YMCA building.
Courtesy of the Maybrook Railroad
Historical Society.

Left: A Central New England blueprint with the YMCA. Courtesy of the
Maybrook Railroad Historical Society
and Doug Barbiero.

Above: The YMCA sign.
Courtesy of the Maybrook Railroad
Historical Society.

CHAPTER FIVE
Railroad Employees

THE YARDMASTER would give orders to a conductor in the classification yard, who was in charge of moving cars to specific tracks. Once the classification was completed with the train assembled, the cars were then routed to the departure yard with the caboose and the engine attached and waiting for travel orders. The conductor held a low executive position but earned more money than the brakeman. Thus, brakemen often studied the rules of the road, rail laws, and codes to qualify for the position of a conductor. The conductor usually had two brakemen under him. One of the brakeman, known as the headman, was responsible for moving the engine around. The other, known as the field man, was responsible for coupling the cars in the classification yard, or field, and helping to pull the train into the departure yard. The yard conductor was in charge of the brakeman, engineer, and fireman. Besides the yard conductors, there were traveling freight conductors and passenger train conductors. The conductor held the waybills that listed each train car's cargo and destination.

Stationed on the footboards or in the engine cab, the head brakeman, or headman, led the engine from one track to another. In the lot, the field man assisted the headman in throwing the switches, which routed the engine onto another track. Also, riding at the rear of a train with many cars, the field man threw the switch to pick up more cars from another track. The yard brakeman assisted in connecting and disconnecting cars. The flagman, a rear brakeman, knew all the call signals, short or long whistles (steam locomotives), and horn blasts (diesel locomotive). This was important during train movement and in emergency situations. For a freight train, the crew generally consisted of four men, including the conductor and his assistant, the brakeman, and the locomotive engineer and his assistant, the fireman. Larger trains often had two or more brakeman stationed at the front and the rear of the train. Passenger trains had an additional crewman, the baggage master. It was essential for a conductor to have a brakeman's knowledge and experience of tools, equipment, and flag and lantern signals. Signals were used for many purposes, including regulating the direction and speed of a train and for emergency notification of an oncoming train. Brakemen inspected and lined the hundreds of railroad switches, each a vital link to a train car move-

Left: Central New England Engine 501 with conductor and crew.
Courtesy of the Maybrook Railroad Historical Society

Right: A Penn Central diesel-electric locomotive with Conductor Bill Shields and Brakeman Slim Layton.
Courtesy of Peter C. McLachlan, photographer

ment within the terminal. Most trains had more than one brake—they usually had one at the front and one at the back, and thus had more than one brakeman. The front and rear brakemen had similar but different responsibilities. The rear brakeman was also the flagman who used the signal flag during the day to warn trains approaching on the same track. The front brakeman lead the engine to different tracks and gave signals to the engineer to go forward or backup. On freight trains he protected the front of the train in case of an emergency. At night, brakemen used a colored lantern to signal other trains. The job of the hump brakeman was to guide railroad cars to designated tracks in the classification yard. The brakeman mounted the railroad car at the crest of the hill, released its brake, and let the car go down the tracks by gravity. Approaching the designated track, the brakeman slowed the car and hitched it to the cars ahead. In the 1940s, brakemen earned about forty or fifty cents less per day than the conductor did. Brakemen had to be very skilled in the use of lanterns and flags, knowing the specific motions to signal speed up, move forward, stop, reduce speed, and release air brakes.

Inspectors in the receiving yards sent railroad cars in need of repairs, parts, or maintenance to the car shop. The car shop was the largest operation in the Maybrook terminal. Among its departments were the painting department, the blacksmith department, and one involved in the cleaning of air brakes. For proper maintenance, a car's air brakes were usually cleaned every three years. Cars that were in a train wreck were rebuilt from the bottom up if enough parts were salvageable. Car shop carpenters were sent out to repair the siding or roof of rail yard sheds. Other car shop employees assisted in the car inspections, always looking to fix a defect that might cause a train wreck. At the terminal's height of

Railroad Employees

employment, during World War II, some five hundred employees worked directly or indirectly for the car shop. This was approximately one third of the labor force in the Maybrook yard at that time. The car shop had a chief clerk and a clerical staff. Each department had a foreman and his assistants, who were called leaders.

The terminal's three major buildings, the enginehouse/roundhouse, the car shop, and the administration building, were spread out over a huge area. Most of the employees lived locally and walked to and from work. It was approximately a half-mile from the administration building to the roundhouse and engine shop. The terminal was divided into three important areas of operation. One third of the operation was clerical staff stationed in the administration building, the YMCA, the car shop, and the enginehouse/roundhouse. Another third of the operation was the repair staff, who were stationed in the enginehouse-roundhouse, and the car shop. (The enginehouse and the car shop were connected together on one side.) The last third of the operation was the yard staff. The original main office building was much smaller than the later administration building, but it had a staff of about four dozen people. The size of staff before the Great Depression was very large, which indicated a period of prosperity during the

The crew by a steam engine.

Brakeman and flagman by the cabooses.

Both courtesy of the Maybrook Railroad Historical Society

Railroad Employees

Facing page
Top: The car shop gang. Left: Brakemen between rail cars. Right: Atop the eastbound hump with Brakeman James Wade. This page
Top: The car shop with passenger car and caboose. Charles Davis Sr., photographer Above: The administration building. Right middle: Tending the rail switches. Bottom: Walking to the administration building. All courtesy of the Maybrook Railroad Historical Society

The main office staff, c. 1927. Courtesy of the Maybrook Railroad Historical Society

1920s. This was due, in part, to the Maybrook yard offering freight services to other railroad companies such as the Ontario & Western. Under the control of the New York, New Haven & Hartford Railroad, the terminal began to phase out passenger service during this time period and concentrated on freighting services.

The trainmaster was in charge of the railroad yard, and all employees were accountable to him either directly or indirectly. Working out of the administration building, he was responsible for making sure that all trains left on schedule from the eastbound departure yard and then from the westbound departure yard. During World War II, troop trains carrying arms and military equipment, as well as prisoners of war from Europe, came through Maybrook, greatly increasing the yard's workload. The staff was increased, and the hours of operation were extended. By the middle of the war, the clerical department had approximately 150 employees to service the thousands of cars that passed through the yard. Along with the trainmaster, the administrative staff included other executives and agents who assisted in processing cars. Responsibilities were divided among those who were in charge of receiving freight and those who were in charge of shipping freight. The general chairman and other executives of the New York, New Haven & Hartford Railroad visited Maybrook to meet with the trainmaster and agents. Even in the 1940s, the switchboard was a large operation. The main switchboard operator was in charge of taking and relaying information that came into the yard by telephone and getting an outside operator or dis-

Railroad Employees

patcher. During this period, Mary Duffy was that key person. Stationed in the administration building, she took a message and then got in touch with the correct shop, office, or person. Located in the middle of the rail yard, her office was a long walk from the village of Maybrook. Administrative clerks were responsible for orders for the westbound and eastbound movement. During the early 1900s, the clerk position was usually given to men, not women. There were very few women working on the railroad until World War II. This changed because of the shortage of men as a result of the draft.

The Central New England Railway built its office around 1900. It was located at the east end of Main Street in Maybrook. The building was used until the mid-1920s when it was abandoned and moved across East Main Street to become a coat factory, Brook May, which specialized in woolen coats. In 1914 the CNE began to expand and built a new administrative office with clerical staffing rooms. The new building was located inside the rail yard and was more accessible for the employees.

The roundhouse and enginehouse each had its own employees including a clerical staff. The agents were in charge of keeping a list of manifests

The trainmaster Thomas Teggan and his replacement, George McBride.

Railroad executives, c. 1940s.

The general chairman and the agents, c.1940s.

All courtesy of the Maybrook Railroad Historical Society

Above: The roundhouse gang, c. pre-1920s. Below: The switchboard operator, Mary Duffy. Right: Central New England administrative building, pre-1920s. Right, bottom: The Central New England Railroad main office staff, c. 1921. All courtesy of the Maybrook Railroad Historical Society

Railroad Employees

Above: On a steam locomotive, c. 1930s.

Left: Harry Dawson, chief clerk of the roundhouse.

Courtesy of the Maybrook Railroad Historical Society

and time sheets for the receiving and departure yards at their desks—the eastbound desk and the westbound desk. Working under the chief clerks were lower clerks whose job was to make up the waybills for the trains. By the 1940s, telephone lines ran throughout many parts of the rail yard including the enginehouse. The roundhouse/enginehouse of the Central New England Railway had a crew of about three dozen employees. They included clerks and a foreman as well as blacksmiths,

boilermakers, welders, and other specialists. By the 1930s, freight train servicing had become the main business of the Maybrook terminal, and the number of enginehouse/roundhouse workers had increased to nearly ninety. These workers varied in age from those in their fifties to young boys in their mid-teens. Most of the young men in the village of Maybrook worked for the railroad, as many of their fathers were employed in the various shops and buildings. The terminal was the major employer in the community until the 1950s, when the coat company, Brook May, hired many residents. After the New York, New Haven & Hartford Railroad had taken over the terminal, it expanded some buildings, created new facilities, and added machinery and workers. More than two dozen employees made up the clerical staff of the enginehouse. By the 1950s, the enginehouse and roundhouse together employed between four hundred and five hundred workers. The foreman and assistant foreman not only repaired but also washed, cleaned, and fully inspected engines and boilers. Fresh water was added to the engine tank from the pipes by the coal trestle. For engine wheel traction, the workers used the sand pipe to fill the sand compartment. Another job at the roundhouse was emptying the ashes into the ash pit while filling up the tender with coal and sand.

Facing page, clockwise from the top:
The grand opening of the Whiting Hoist, c. 1924.
Car shop workers with equipment on a gondola flatcar.
Tresstle workers at Millbrook.
At the roundhouse and engine house, c. 1950s.
The engine house gang, c.1950s.
Crewmen from the car shop.
All courtesy of the Maybrook Railroad Historical Society

Behind the roundhouse and the car shop was a large tank that held gas, which was piped into the car shop and roundhouse and used for welding and cutting metal.

In the 1930s and part of the 1940s, the repair crew was referred to as the "maintenance of way crew." During the 1940s to the 1970s in the Maybrook yard, this group of about seven to as many as ten employees were called the "section gang." The maintenance of way crew consisted of a foreman, a welder, a motorcar operator, and laborers. These crewmen worked throughout the rail yard making repairs. They had a motorcar that was able to tow a small flatbed carrying rails, spikes, shovels, jacks, and other track repair and maintenance equipment. Sometimes the crew went with the road gang and a truck to do outside repairs, particularly if a wreck had occurred, necessitating extra manpower. Sometimes workers from the car shop were assigned to assist a maintenance of way crew if they were in need of a welder. The "section gang" maintained all the tracks within the rail yard and outside the yard. Some of the jobs were to replace or repair the tie plates, and then a "grinder" smoothed the weld even to the surface of the plate.

When cargo arrived at the rail yard, it was unloaded from the boxcars onto platforms or docks. There, it was inspected and reassigned to other cars or loaded onto trucks to be delivered within the region. The three-man "transfer gang" worked on a long platform about the length of two long buildings with boxcars on each side. The highest paid of the three men was the checker who received about twenty cents more an hour than the loader during the 1950s The trucker was the lowest paid of the three employees. Experience and time would promote the trucker to a loader and finally, a checker. The trucker took boxes off one car, placed them on a handcart, and

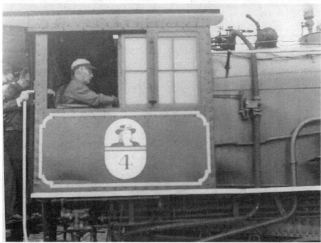

This page
Top: Platform group. Above, left: Locomotive cab. Right: Loading platform.

Facing page
Top left: The silent partners, Mel Fetter and Otis Cobleigh. Top right: The maintenance of way gang, c. 1950s.
Bottom: April safety meeting platform group.

Courtesy of the Maybrook Railroad Historical Society

then wheeled them over to the designated boxcar. The loader or stevedore took the cargo and placed it in the designated boxcar. The checker remained with the initial boxcar and marked off all cargo taken from the original boxcar that the trucker then stacked. In 1953, the stevedore made about seven to eight dollars per day. One of the jobs of the transfer gang was to keep the cargo stacked level and at a certain height on each boxcar, especially

Maybrook railroad station.
Courtesy of the Maybrook Railroad Historical Society

the open cars and gondolas. Sometimes a platform crew stacked old rail ties that the maintenance of way gang replaced with new ties. These ties lasted for twenty to thirty years on average. The men at the platform were called "stackers," as they lifted and placed these eight to nine foot ties together. Sometimes the ties would be as long as sixteen feet. These were used for the switches. Four men used tie tongs to carry the ties.

The Maybrook Railroad terminal did have a railroad station. This was located at the south end of Main Street. When the Central New England Railroad owned the railroad terminal during the early decades of the twentieth century, both passenger and freight service were part of the rail service of the company. There was one room inside the station and an outside toilet. Behind the railroad station was the old CNE administrative office. Many local residents took the train from Maybrook to Poughkeepsie.

The departure of the train occurred when the waybills arrived from the clerical department in the administration building. The engineer, fireman (unless it was a diesel engine), conductor, and front brakeman waited in the cab of the locomotive. Often, some boxcars or flatcars remained in the terminal so that later, incoming cargo could be added for shipment. The delivery of the orders from a clerk in the departure yard was the final phase. "Grabbing orders on the fly" meant that the train was in motion as the clerk handed the waybills or destination orders to the conductor.

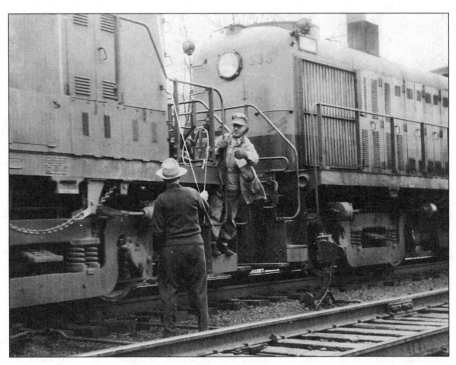

Grabbing orders on the fly.
Courtesy of the Maybrook Railroad Historical Society
and Peter C. McLachlan, photographer

CHAPTER SIX
Railroad Machines

THERE were many machines throughout the rail yard. Some were large machines used inside the car shop, enginehouse, roundhouse, etc. Aside from these, the rail yard had motorized and nonmotorized vehicles that were used for transportation, hauling, and lifting rail material. In the years before the small switch engine, the "pump car" was used. The pump car handle went up and down moving gears to the wheels. The handle provided the means for movement in the years before the use of the gasoline engine motor car. Usually two men pushed the handle. A small crew of men rode on the platform and stepped off to repair a railroad tie, track, or switch. The pump car was considered fast and effective for getting repairmen out on the line or around the rail yard. The motorcar was transportation for the signal department or maintenance of way gang to go from one area to another in the rail yard. They usually had orders from the dispatcher. Sometimes the orders would be taken to the siding after letting freight trains go by. The motor car was a gasoline engine vehicle and was used to transport two to eight workers in and around the yard. The car was also used to transport rails and ties, rather than using half dozen or more men to carry them. The motorcar replaced the old hand pump cars. There were other types of mechanized vehicles such as the switcher engines that transported rail cars from nearby sidings or depots.

The "big hook" was part of the machinery and tools of the car shop in the rail yard. A designated crew used the hook to lift, and then lower onto the track, engines or cars that were off or partially on the track. The big hook was also used to remove cars and engines from a train wreck and to lift large debris off the track. Train wrecks were part of daily life. Over the years, there have been many different causes for wrecks and derailments, among them, an obstruction on the tracks, a damaged railroad tie or track, and faulty air brakes or a train traveling at a high speed on a sharp curve. The big hook had several hooks and a steel harness to fit around the body of a car or engine. The apparatus was used to lift cars from a train wreck and place them on the rail track or a flatbed to be taken back to the car shop for salvaging, parts, or repair. Those cars that were beyond repair were stripped of parts that could be used on other cars. Prior to lifting the engine, a cable attached the front and rear to the big hook to balance the weight.

The wrecking master was in charge of the hook and gave orders to the wrecking crew. The wrecking crew consisted of two dozen workers from the car shop and the rail yard. Using signals, the wrecking master directed the engineer on the crane of the hook that was moving the engine. With the wrecking master and the hook engineer was a clerk who took charge of the car's content, and a fireman who quelled any flames or fire the engine created.

Another lifting device was the "clam digger." The clam digger was used in making a track bed to put more tracks into the rail yard. The gravel and dirt as well as ashes from the ash pit were used to spread a new foundation base for a track bed for rail and ties. The New York, New Haven & Hartford Railroad used this when it took control of the Central New England Railroad during the 1920s. It was during this time that the number of tracks increased to accommodate more traffic on both the westbound and eastbound yards.

The machine shop was located behind the engine dispatcher's office, and it was also where men had their lockers during the period of the 1920s. Parts were tooled and made for the steam engines. The machine shop

The hand pump car.

Motorcar for maintenance of way gang.

Clam digger with gondola car and gravel.

Opposite page: The big hook.

The East Walden train wreck.

Lifting a New Haven diesel engine.

All courtesy of the Maybrook Railroad Historical Society

Railroad Machines

workers ground down the wheels of the cars to make sure there were no flat spots. Located in the long enginehouse building, where the steam engines were serviced, these giant grindstones and massive machines were able to build many of the iron and steel parts of the train.

Switcher engines brought railroad cars either from Campbell Hall to Maybrook or from Poughkeepsie to Maybrook and back. Campbell Hall was a terminal the New York Central Railroad used. The New York, New Haven & Hartford agreed to have the Maybrook yard repair some of the New York Central cars, and those cars had to be towed to Maybrook and then returned to Campbell Hall for the New York Central to pick up. The switcher engine helped transport the small cranes to be used in or outside the rail yard.

The Maybrook road engine.
Below: The Poughkeepsie switcher.
Both courtesy of the Maybrook Railroad Historical Society

CHAPTER SEVEN
Railroad Tools and Equipment

THERE WERE MANY TOOLS that were used inside the rail yard, especially by the maintenance of way gang, brakemen, conductors, inspectors, fireman, flagmen, etc. Some of the essential materials for the railroad cars and engines were the tie, rail spike, and rail plate. The rail of iron and steel sat on a firm bed of gravel and wood (ties). Tie carriers worked in conjunction with rail carriers. Six men could carry the large ties, about seven feet in length. They placed the ties parallel on a crushed stone bed. Once the ties were leveled and the tie plates put down, the rail carriers laid the rail on top of several ties. These rails weighed about one thousand to eighteen thousand pounds, depending on the length of the section. Then, spikes were driven in to secure the rail and tie. A shoulder on each spike gripped the base of the rail as each spike was driven through a hole in the tie plate. There were four spikes on each tie plate, two on each side. (Some larger plates had three on each side.) The holes on a tie plate were spaced about five inches apart.

Shovels and forks were used for various purposes in the rail yard and on the train. Firemen on trains used the coal scoop shovel. These shovels were about four feet in length with a short handle. They were sometimes given nicknames, such as "hand bombers" or "banjos." The scoop, or mouth of the shovel, was wide and deep for bits and chunks of coal that firemen shoveled into the firebox to get the steam pressure up. They were used on trains that did not have stokers. The ballast fork had several different purposes. The track crew used this fork to remove stone in the roadbed underneath the ties and the rails. The icehouse crew used it to shovel or move crushed ice into the refrigerator boxcars. Several yard departments used it as a universal tool, and most of the sheds or shanties had one. Rail switches had to be kept clear so that they could be thrown, or shifted, to move trains, engines, or cars from one track to another. Because the switches became inoperable under heavy snow or ice, boys from the village (hired in the early years) and the local track gang had to shovel them out. Many high school boys, fifteen to seventeen, took time off from school and reported as part-time workers in the rail yard to shovel snow. Large snowstorms and ice storms were normal weather conditions in Orange County where the Maybrook terminal was located.

The brake shoe was used on all rail cars and engines. Every rail vehicle, regardless of type, had at least two brake shoes and usually

70 | The Railroad Switching Terminal

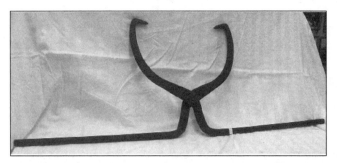

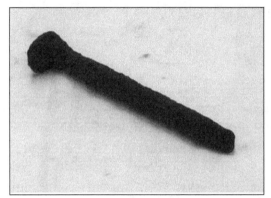

This page
Clockwise from top left: A tie carrier. A two-man rail carrier. An air hose. A coal scoop shovel. A rail with a tie plate. A railroad spike.

Opposite page
Clockwise from the top: A ballast fork. A marker lamp. A snow shovel for switches. An air brake handle. Railroad brake shoes.

All courtesy of the Maybrook Railroad Historical Society and Dan Green, photographer

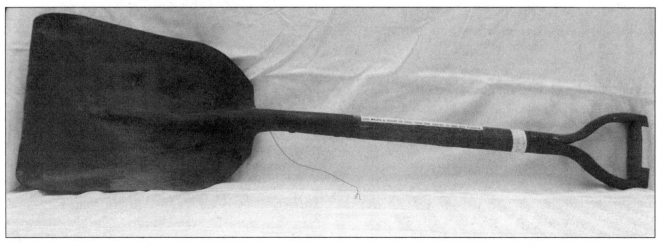

Railroad Tools and Equipment 71

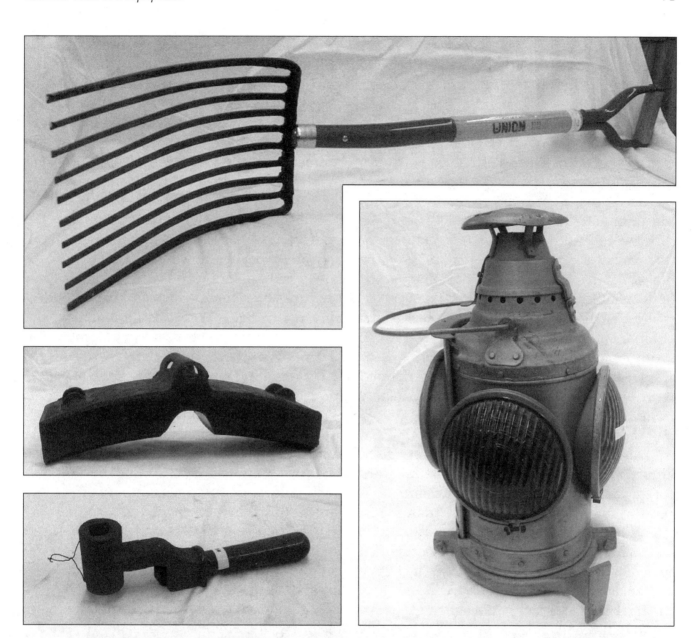

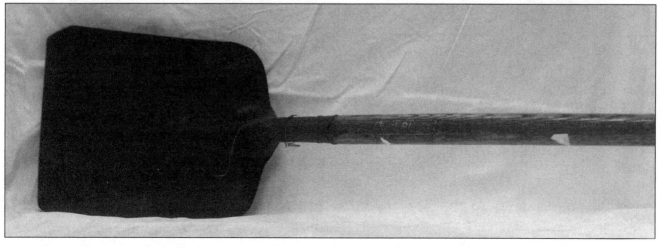

one for each wheel. In the early days, the shoes were cast in iron. Brake shoes became worn down during the miles of travel and numerous stops. Then, they had to be replaced. Newer brake shoes, made from a composite of materials, weighed a quarter of the old shoes. Brake handles helped to control the train by letting air out of the cylinders of the cars. Used if necessary in connection with the air brakes, the handles were located in the caboose and in the engine. The conductor or flagman in the rear and the engineer or the brakeman in the front of the train operated the brake handles.

The air hose was an essential part of the equipment on every car and train. Before the train moved, hoses at each end of every car were connected and the train was charged with air to bring the pressure up to ninety pounds. Then, the air brakes were released and the train got under way.

Different lights and lanterns were used either on the railroad cars or in the rail yard for various reasons. A red reflector lamp was used to mark the rear car of the train, while the amber light indicated that the last car, the caboose, was occupied and could not be tied on to another railroad car. This lamp had three amber reflectors and one reflector glass.

Track switches each had a light and/or target to indicate the route condition. Generally a green light meant that the switch was aligned for straight through running while a red light indicated that the switch was in the curved or diverging position. The targets were painted in bright colors for daylight visibility and were illuminated by kerosene lights at night. The lights were mechanically linked to turn when the switch position was changed. Red and green lights on towers or overhead bridges were used for main line train control much like traffic lights are used at road intersection.

At night, floodlights were used throughout the Maybrook terminal to light up the yard and the enginehouse area. The bulbs ranged from 500 watts to 1,000 watts. The lights were turned on manually, as there were no light controllers at the time. Because the railroad had its own powerhouse, which took over when the power went out, the floodlights were always available. Inspectors used portable carbide lights to illuminate the undercarriage of each car that entered the arrival or departure yards. The lights contained carbide and water, which combined to produce acetylene gas, which burned with a very bright light. With this illumination, the inspectors examined the safety equipment, the air lines, the wheels, and other areas to ensure that everything was in fine to excellent condition. They sent any car with a visible problem directly to the car shop.

During the mid-1940s, battery lights replaced carbide lights. Inspectors used these lights to examine arriving and departing cars and engines for any defects. Another light or lantern that was used on the train was the passenger train light. This small light was used for giving signals on a passenger train. The conductor, the trainman, and the ticket collector each used it for different purposes. A functional light, it was used to signal others, including the engineer ahead, to inspect the train, or to light the way. Before the 1960s, whistle, light, lantern, or flag accomplished communication from one end of the train to the other. Lights or lanterns were used to give specific signals, for example, stop, move forward, and move backward. Developed for safety reasons, these signals were incorporated in the rules that rail employees had to study and memorize.

Another assortment of tools were the various wrenches that were used in the rail yard or in the car shop. The joint bolt wrench was

Railroad Tools and Equipment

Above, clockwise from the left: The main line light. A rail yard floodlight. An inspector's carbide light. An inspector's battery lights. A passenger train light. Below, clockwise from top left: A steel-forged hammer. A joint bolt wrench. A signal light. Car repair wrenches. A rail spike puller. A two-pound sledgehammer. A rail-spiking mallet. In the center: A car jack. All courtesy of the Maybrook Railroad Historical Society and Dan Green, photographer

one of these wrenches. Large bolts went directly through the rails and fish plates tying them together at the joints. The maintenance crews inspected the bolts, tie plates, and ties along the three to five miles of rail in the Maybrook yard and around its perimeter. When a bolt was causing problems, the large bolt wrench was used to extract it and to replace it with a new one. Members of the crew used the rail spike puller to remove a spike from the plate and tie so that it could be repaired. Approximately five feet in length and fifty pounds in weight, it pulled the spike out of the plate. Trainmen and inspectors carried car repair wrenches in their toolbox and used them in the car shop and the rail yard. When any equipment needed to be changed, the wrenches served as the universal tool. They were used on air hoses and air cocks. The car jack was used to help move a rail car or a heavy piece of equipment in the car repair shop or at the scene of a wreck. Operated with a crowbar, the jack lifted objects vertically. In later years, an air-powered jack replaced the car jack.

Another common tool used in various shops in the rail yard were hammers, some of which were produced in the rail yard. Sledgehammers, such as the two-pound model, were used in diesel engines and cabooses. Similar to the steel-forged hammers, these hammers were used for jobs that required greater pounding power. They were used in many of the shops in both the enginehouse and the car shop, and especially in the blacksmith shop.

Steel-forged hammers were used for work on diesels and cabooses. The railroads forged and made them in the blacksmith shop. Used mostly for heavy-duty pounding, these hammers could break wire and split cotter keys. Track crews putting down new rail used rail-spiking mallets to drive the spikes into the ties. The men usually worked in pairs, driving spikes on alternate strokes. Each man had his own mallet and took turns hitting the spike until it was seated all the way into the tie plate. The spike mallet has a very small head, approximately the same diameter as the head of the spike.

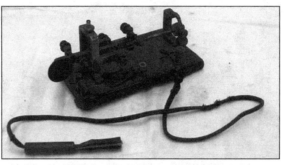

A telegraph key. A railroad air whistle. Both courtesy of the Maybrook Railroad Historical Society and Dan Green, photographer

There were many different means of communication in the rail yard and outside the rail yard. For nearly a century, the telegraph was the main form of communication. Morse Code was sent over a copper wire, which was strung from New Haven, Connecticut, to Maybrook and from Maybrook to the dispatchers of other railroads. Later, telephones were located throughout the yard system and along the freight line. The telephone bell sounded different rings for particular people and purposes.

Aside from the telephone and telegraph, whistles were another means of communication. The railroad air whistle was mounted in the departure yard. The air whistle was used during severe weather such as heavy fog. It notified the engineer to set the brakes on the train prior to leaving the rail yard. The air brakes had to be tested to make sure that the air pressure was up.

Railroad Tools and Equipment

**A communication telephone. A signal whistle for passenger service. The engine warning bell.
All courtesy of the Maybrook Railroad Historical Society and Dan Green, photographer**

The locomotive steam whistle was the form of railroad communications in use before radio and telephone. It was located on the top of the locomotive boiler and was loud enough to be heard for miles in any direction. The engineer controlled the whistle and used it to signal the crew when starting or backing the train or in emergency situations. It was also used while running on the main line to warn the local population at grade crossings. These signals are still in use on diesel trains with loud horns. Another smaller whistle in the locomotive was used as a warning device to alert the engineer and the fireman that it was time to add water to the engine. If water was not added, the steam engine could blow up. The bell at the front of the steam locomotive rang to alert the rail yard that the train was approaching, as well as to clear the tracks ahead of any wandering livestock. The headlight below the bell was used at night to illuminate the tracks, show any obstructions ahead, and give an idea of position to any oncoming trains. The steel gate at the bottom of the front platform was originally much wider and triangular in shape, similar to a ram. Known as a cowcatcher, it was a useful device to clear the tracks of debris or livestock. The engine bell rang mostly as an alert. It was used to get the attention of the crew when the engine was standing still. It had specific rings for signaling the forward and backward movements of the engine. At a railroad crossing, it rang as a warning that the train was approaching. Steam locomotive trains at the turn of the century had a large illuminating light at the head of the train, but many did not have the engine bell. As steam trains approached towns, the engineer or the front brakeman pulled the rope that rang the huge bell at the front and top of the locomotive. Heard far and wide, the very loud bell announced the arriving train. When the diesel engine replaced the old steam locomotive, large horns mounted on top of the engine replaced the engine bell. To this day, these large horns announce their presence, as well as their arrival, at railroad crossings.

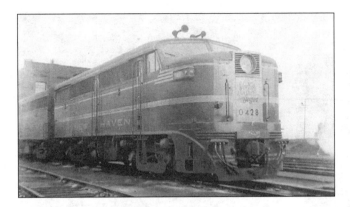

Top: A diesel locomotive with twin engine horns.

Above: Railroad boys on a steam locomotive with engine warning bell.

Both courtesy of the Maybrook Railroad Historical Society

Inspectors had a variety of tools that they carried in a special toolbox. The car inspector's job was to walk an arriving or departing train to ensure that all its safety equipment was functional and any last minute repairs were done. Inspectors carried tool boxes containing an assortment of hand tools such as an open-end wrench and pry bar, which were used to examined the brake shoes. Inspectors used the journal-box hook, sometimes referred to as the knifing tool, to lift the cover of the journal box. Once the box was opened, they checked to see that the brass slide was in service or serviceable and that it was properly oiled and not overheated. The hook was used in the shop and in the yard. To keep the bearings lubricated, the journal box was packed with shredded material that had been soaked in sixty-weight oil. This journal box oil lubricated the brass slide on top of the axle. Longneck oilcans were used during the days of the steam engine. When the engine came to a stop, the engineer got out of the cab with his oil can full of lubricant and oiled every moving metal part on all sides of the steam engine, especially the rods and wheels. This lessened the wear and tear on the engine. These oil cans had a small thumb-operated pump. They were used later on diesel locomotives but not as often. Before the time of battery-operated lights, the engineer used a kerosene torch to give off light for inspecting the steam engine. The torch also was used to thaw any lines that had frozen after being exposed to extreme cold.

Railroad workers generally wore a hat, jacket, and bib overalls. Pockets in the jacket and overalls allowed for carrying small equipment, pencils, pens, paper, cards, and so on. This was typical of the employees of the freighting service, especially the engineer and the brakeman. Passenger service employees wore a black uniform.

To obtain more braking power, a club was

Railroad Tools and Equipment

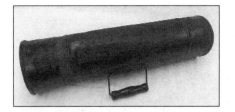
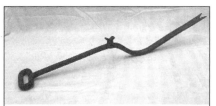

Above, clockwise from top left: An inspector's toolbox. A journal box hook. Journal box-packing material. A kerosene torch. A long-neck oilcan.

Right: The brakemen's club. Below: A hat and uniform.

All courtesy of the Maybrook Railroad Historical Society and Dan Green, photographer

often used when applying the manual staff brakes. Staff brakes were very hard to operate. By turning the spokes of the wheel (above the boxcar) with the brake club, more leverage was gained. This was an essential tool for brakemen riding the boxcar on the eastbound or westbound humps and helped to slow the cars down.

The brakeman, engineer, fireman, and conductor all were required to know the rules of the road. To qualify

 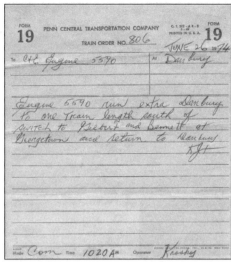 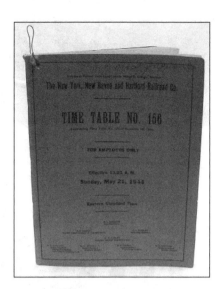

Left: Rule book. Right: The timetable book.
Both courtesy of the Maybrook Railroad Historical Society and Dan Green, photographer
Middle: Form 19 train order. Courtesy of George Birch, the George Birch Railroad Collection

for their positions, newly hired brakemen had forty-five days to learn their section of the rules. The flagmen had the next ninety days to learn their part. Conductors and engineers had to know the entire book of rules.

The timetable book listed all of the Class A, or Class 1, passenger trains and all the train schedules for the passenger service. It included information on train stations, services, rights of way, speeds, and operation. Train crewmen kept a copy of the book in a pocket, as well as in the caboose.

Form 19 was a train order. The dispatcher, who was contacted by telephone or radio, sent this. It was composed and read back to him before he initialed it to be processed. At the bottom was the dispatcher's name and the time and date. When there was no schedule, the trains ran "Extra." The train was sent to a specific point and could not proceed farther than the destination on the train order. Trains would leave Maybrook and go to different destinations in Connecticut. Some would go to Bridgeport, Hartford, Waterbury, Danbury, and New Haven. At Cedar Hill trains were classified and dispatched toward farther destinations, west and east. These orders were given to divert the engine or train to a siding to wait until train traffic passed a specific point. To initiate the train order, the engineer needed a Form A clearance form. The form indicated the time the dispatcher sanctioned the order. The clearance form was given to the

Form A clearance form. Courtesy of George Birch, the George Birch Railroad Collection

Railroad Tools and Equipment

A trainman's hat plate and a ticket collector's hat plate.
Courtesy of the Maybrook Railroad Historical Society and Dan Green, photographer

engineer from the operator at the tower. A copy was given to both the conductor and the engineer. This was standard form in all rail yards of the New York, New Haven & Hartford Railroad. Signals controlled Maybrook traffic, but if the signals failed, these forms were the backup system for movement out of the rail yard eastbound or westbound.

There were various small tools and equipment for both the freighting service and the passenger service. Passenger service trainmen stayed outside with the conductor to make certain that everyone was either on or off the train. The trainmen gave the engineer the signal to move or pull out of the station. Signals were passed from the conductor to the ticket collector to the brakeman to highball, or proceed, to the next station.

On passenger trains, conductors and ticket collectors punched tickets with a ticket punch. Long skeleton keys were used to enter cabooses, which were padlocked, and smaller keys were used to open doors or compartments that stored passengers' items. Generally, every switch on the main line was locked and secured with switch locks as a precautionary measure to prevent tampering. Occasionally, switch locks were used in the yard on those switches that were to be thrown only when unlocked.

There was a wide range of miscellaneous equipment. Tie nails were put in the center of the ties. At the head of the tie nail was an engraved date with the last two numbers for the year. That date let the track crew know how old the ties were and which should be replaced because of age. When new ties were put into the tie bed, maintenance of way crewmen put in tie nails to indicate the new date.

Matchboxes were mass-produced especially for the railroad. The common wooden matchbox held dozens of matchsticks. The

Top: Ticket punches. A caboose key and switch keys.
Above: Padlocks, switch locks and keys.
Both courtesy of the Maybrook Railroad Historical Society and Dan Green, photographer

Clockwise from the top left: Tie nails. A railroad matchbox. Supply tags and baggage tags. Railroad identification tags. An ice stamp. Courtesy of the Maybrook Railroad Historical Society and Dan Green, photographer

match ignited when struck on the abrasive strip on the side of the box. Railroad matchsticks were longer than conventional household matches, as a longer shaft was needed to reach the wick of the lantern. They were used to light the kerosene-filled signal lights in the caboose, the marker lights, the switch lanterns, and other lights.

The ice stamp was a rubber stamp used to indicate that the refrigerator cars had been re-iced at the Maybrook yard. The waybills of each refrigerator car that came into the yard showed the date of the last re-icing. The Maybrook icehouse manager stamped the waybill with the new re-icing date.

Tags were used for both freight service and passenger service. In the early days of rail service, as passengers boarded a train, a porter tagged their baggage. The bags were then either stored in special compartments or taken directly to a private cabin or other accommodation. The tag letter and number were recorded along with the name of the owner and the railroad station or train car destination. Supply tags were inventoried and registered to make sure all of them were returned after use. Seals were used on railroad cars. Freight was loaded into a boxcar in the same way it is today into a tractor trailer. The seals were then placed on the door and remained intact until the railroad car arrived at its destination. They were used on any compartment—boxcar, tanker car, or refrigerator car.

The railroad employees at the Maybrook terminal used identification tags during World War II, from 1942 to 1945. Because of fear of potential espionage by agents of Imperial Japan or Nazi Germany, a railroad detective checked the tags as employees came and went.

There were neckerchiefs that were souvenirs or commemorative items symbolizing the unity of the Brotherhood of Railroad Workers. Such bandannas were worn around the neck to protect against windburn or rashes from working near furnaces in the shops or on the engines. They were also used as a face mask to prevent inhaling of fumes and smoke from the steam engines or smoke and gas from the workshops. Although many chose not to wear them, the bandannas were a functional, but not mandatory part, of railroad dress.

Railroad Tools and Equipment

Railroad company logo buttons, 1899–present. Left to right:
1899-1927 Central New England, 1927-1969 NYNH & Hartford, 1969-1976 Penn Central, 1976- Conrail.
Courtesy of the Maybrook Railroad Historical Society and Dan Green, photographer

The Central New England Railway established the Maybrook Switching Terminal after the Poughkeepsie Bridge was constructed. The small switching terminal became the largest in the Northeast in the pre-1920s era. The New York, New Haven & Hartford Railroad's acquisition of the Central New England led to the expansion of the terminal and the number of trains that could be serviced on a daily basis. The forced merger of the New York Central, the Pennsylvania, and the New Haven railroads into the ill-fated Penn Central in the early 1970s and the 1974 Poughkeepsie bridge fire led to the eventual closing of the Maybrook terminal. By the mid 1970s Conrail had taken over from the failed Penn Central and began to discontinue unprofitable rail lines and terminals in the eastern United States while maintaining, many in the Midwest and West. Much of the traffic that formerly passed through Maybrook was routed farther north to Selkirk Yard and the Hudson River bridge near Albany.

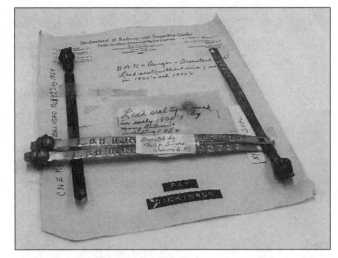

Right top: Railroad car seals.

Right: A railroad neckerchief.

Courtesy of the Maybrook Railroad Historical Society and Dan Green, photographer

CHAPTER EIGHT
In and Around the Rail Yard

RAILROAD WORKERS created various organizations and unions to protect their livelihood. After the creation of several transcontinental railroads, including the Central Pacific Railroad, the Union Pacific Railroad, and the Southern Pacific Railroad, as well as numerous small lines throughout the United States, employees created a national union, the American Railway Union. This union was developed toward the end of the nineteenth century under the leadership of Eugene V. Debs. However, railroad brotherhoods had existed before the formation of the American Railway Union. Some brotherhoods had become smaller unions affiliated with the newly created American Federation of Labor in the 1880s. The local lodge in Maybrook was number 813. The members were employees of the rail yard as well as men who worked on the road traveling from Maybrook to Connecticut. The lodge members from out of the area stayed at the local YMCA and attended some of the meetings of the local lodge. Some of the wives and the daughters of railroad workers created a duplicate organization. The Ladies Auxiliary of the Brotherhood of Railroad Workers was created at the Maybrook terminal. Although this was more of a social group, they were very supportive of railroad pensions and disabilities, but they were not railroad employees. They held fundraisers for the local brotherhood. Another volunteer group was the Trustees of the YMCA. All of the men who were trustees were railroad employees. They were agents, trainmasters, wrecking masters, conductors, and engineers. The New York, New Haven & Hartford Railroad owned the YMCA. The rooms and facilities provided were clean from the living quarters to the main dining hall.

Opposite page

Top: Some of the Membership of Lodge #813 of the Brotherhood of Railroad Trainmen, left to right: J. E. Winters, K. L. Halstead, G. Freeman, J. Schoonmaker, A. Birch, S. Henry, G. Carlew, W. Bishop, H. Janville, R. McMann, J. B. Jacobs, D. V. Brown, F. Amodio, E. Holman, S. Dollaway, J. Canade, E. Dalton, F. Ferrado, Standing in back row: P. Marino, A. S. Christiano, and T. Marano.

Bottom: The Maybrook Ladies Auxiliary of the Brotherhood of Railroad Workers, c. 1930s. First row, left to right: Nellie Hawkins, Ethel Treptow, Lucy Bishop, Anna Call, and Mary Bullis. Second row, left to right: Martha Halstead, Sarah Legere, Elinor Thompson, Rose McDonald, Elizabeth Decker, and Eva Evans.

Courtesy of the Maybrook Railroad Historical Society

Trustees for the YMCA. Left to right: Augie Christian, Fred Cole, Carl Eicholtz, and Mr. Rosenberger. Back Row: (Unknown), Bill Teed, Francis Fisher, James Doran, Mr. Cummings, and two additional men from New Haven. Courtesy of the Maybrook Railroad Historical Society

By the 1960s, the rail service at the Maybrook terminal began to compete against local trucking corporations such as Yellow Freight and McLeans well before the Poughkeepsie Bridge fire in the 1970s. The community was no longer a railroad community in which most of the inhabitants worked directly or indirectly for the New York, New Haven & Hartford Railroad.

Last glimpse of the New York, New Haven & Hartford engine and cars, c. 1950s.
Courtesy of the Maybrook Railroad Historical Society

Above: Gondolas with large pipes.
Below: At the beginning, a small rail station.
Both courtesy of the Maybrook Railroad Historical Society

ANOTHER PURPLE MOUNTAIN PRESS RAILROAD TITLE YOU WILL ENJOY

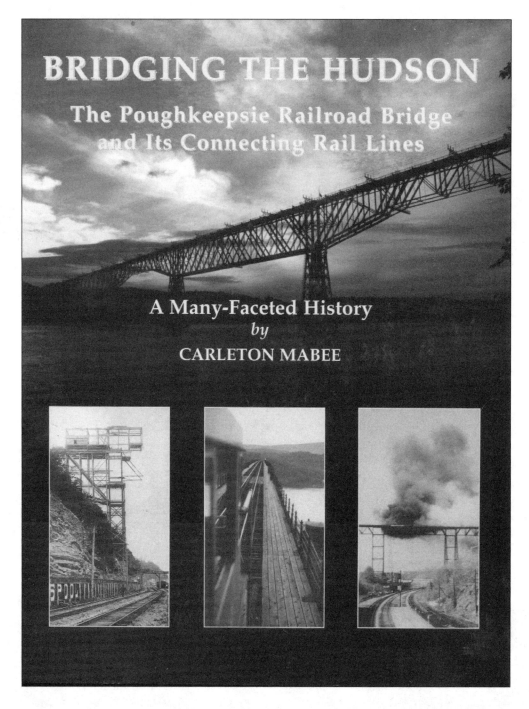

BRIDGING THE HUDSON, by Pulitzer Prize-winning author Carleton Mabee, is a comprehensive history of the Poughkeepsie Railroad Bridge and its connecting rail lines, the first ever published. More oriented to people than technology, the book tells the story of the men who built the bridge and its related lines, and ran trains over them. It tells how maintenance men cared for the bridge, rowers raced under it, hoboes camped under its approaches. It explains why the number of trains crossing the bridge gradually declined, and how after a fire, the bridge was abandoned. It recounts how since then, friends of the bridge have developed imaginative proposals for rehabilitating the bridge for new purposes, proposals which may yet be carried out. 296 pages, paperback, $24.00

ANOTHER PURPLE MOUNTAIN PRESS RAILROAD TITLE YOU WILL ENJOY

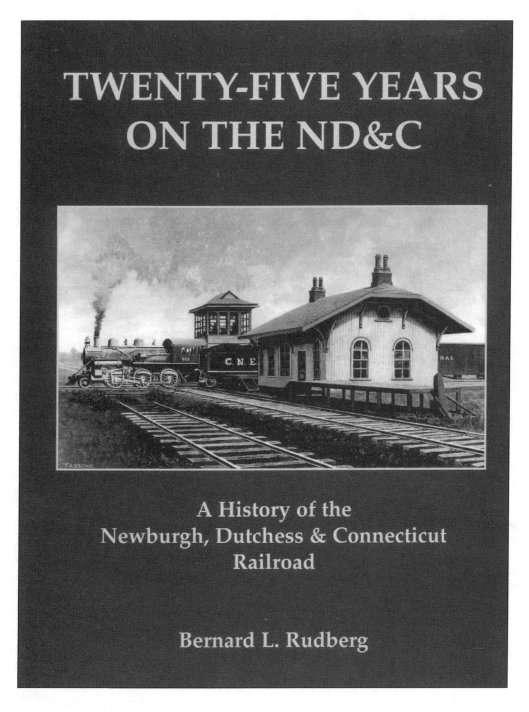

The railroad tracks that ran from Dutchess Junction and Matteawan (Beacon, New York) through Hopewell and Millbrook to Millerton and to Connecticut at State Line had several different names in its first few years of existence. Out of that chaos grew the Newburgh, Dutchess & Connecticut Railroad. The ND&C Railroad under the leadership of John Schultze and Charles Kimball established an operation that survived through good times and bad for over twenty-five years until it was absorbed into the Central New England Railway later becoming part of the New Haven Railroad. Still later, eleven miles of the old ND&C line became part of the ill-fated Penn Central, next Conrail, then the Housatonic Railroad, and currently Metro North. 207 pages, paperback, $22.50

About the Author

MARC NEWMAN is an author with numerous publications to his credit. His works include treatments of the Civil War, the American Revolution, and other historical topics. Aside from his published works, he has been a designer of historical commemoratives and historical playing cards. A well known instructor in New York State, he has been the recipient of national and state awards for his work in the fields of history and historical education.

About the Publisher

PURPLE MOUNTAIN PRESS, established in 1973, publishes books of regional New York State interest. Specialties include colonial history, transportation, and maritime subjects. For a free catalog, write Purple Mountain Press, PO Box 309, Fleischmanns, NY 12430-0309, or call 800-325-2665, or fax 845-254-4476, or email purple@catskill.net. Visit us on the web at www.catskill.net/purple.